Nothing can bring you peace but yourself.

Ralph Waldo Emerson
Self-Reliance

THE SPRINGS OF JOY

by TASHA TUDOR

Rand McNally & Company

Chicago • New York • San Francisco

To F.B.S.

Still the fair vision lives! Say nevermore
That dreams are fragile things. What
    else endures
Of all this broken world save only dreams!

Unknown

Library of Congress Cataloging in Publication Data
Tudor, Tasha.
The springs of joy.

1. Tudor, Tasha. 2. Joy in art. 3. Joy in
literature. I. Title.
NC975.5.T82A4 1979   741.9'73   79-66708
ISBN 0-528-82047-8

In deference to the sensibilities of some readers, the publisher
has deleted several lines from the Walt Whitman poem contained herein.

Foreword

Joy and peace are a state of mind, easy for some to
come by, difficult for others. This book pictures a
few of the things that have brought, and still do
bring, intense joy to me.

This is not a storybook—it has no particular
beginning, no end, and definitely *no message*.
It is merely a statement of delight, drawn from
memory past and present.

May it bring you as much happiness in perusing its
pictures as it has given me in setting them down.

The pictures are my own, the quotations are "other
men's flowers."

Tasha Tudor
Corgi Cottage, 1979

"Life is far too important a thing
to ever talk seriously about."

Oscar Wilde

For out of ourselves we can never pass,
nor can there be in creation what in the
creator was not.

Oscar Wilde
The Critic as Artist

If one advances confidently in the direction of his
dreams, and endeavors to live the life which he has
imagined, he will meet with a success unexpected in
common hours.

Henry David Thoreau
Walden

We are such stuff as dreams are made on ...

William Shakespeare
The Tempest

The happiness of life is made up of minute fractions—the little soon forgotten charities of a kiss or smile, a kind look, a heartfelt compliment, and the countless infinitesimals of pleasurable and genial feeling.

Samuel Taylor Coleridge
The Improvisatore

Solitude is as needful to the imagination
as society is wholesome for the character.

James Russell Lowell
Dryden in *Literary Essays*

Happy the man, and happy he alone,
He who can call today his own;
He who, secure within, can say,
Tomorrow, do thy worst, for I have liv'd today.

John Dryden
Imitation of Horace

...when meadow, grove, and stream,
The earth, and every common sight,
    To me did seem
    Apparell'd in celestial light,
The glory and the freshness of a dream.

William Wordsworth
Ode, Intimations of Immortality

If the day and night be such that you greet them with joy, and life emits a fragrance like flowers and sweet-scented herbs, is more elastic, more immortal—that is your success. All nature is your congratulation, and you have cause momentarily to bless yourself.

Henry David Thoreau
Walden

I, singularly moved
To love the lovely that are not beloved,
Of all the seasons, most
Love Winter, and to trace

The sense of the Trophonian pallor on her face.
It is not death, but plenitude of peace;
And the dim cloud that does the world enfold
Hath less the characters of dark and cold
Than warmth and light asleep,
And correspondent breathing seems to keep
With the infant harvest, breathing soft below
Its eider coverlet of snow.

Coventry Patmore
Winter in *The Unknown Eros*

There are few hours in life more agreeable than
the hour dedicated to the ceremony known as
afternoon tea.

Henry James
Portrait of a Lady

'Tis the good reader that makes the good book;
in every book he finds passages which seem
confidences or asides hidden from all else and
unmistakably meant for his ear; the profit of books
is according to the sensibility of the reader; the
profoundest thought or passion sleeps as in a mine,
until it is discovered by an equal mind and heart.

Ralph Waldo Emerson
Success

What would the world be, once bereft
Of wet and wildness? Let them be left,
O let them be left, wildness and wet,
Long live the weeds and the wildness yet.

Gerard Manley Hopkins
Inversnaid

Be like the bird
That, pausing in her flight
Awhile on boughs too slight,
Feels them give way
Beneath her and yet sings,
Knowing that she hath wings.

Victor Hugo
source unknown

There is no season such delight can bring

As summer, autumn, winter and the spring.

William Browne
source unknown

No heaven can come to us unless our hearts
find rest in it today.
Take heaven.

The gloom of the world is but a shadow;
behind it, yet within our reach, is joy.
Take joy.

Fra Giovanni
source unknown

People are always blaming their circumstances
for what they are. I don't believe in circumstances.
The people who get on in this world are the people
who get up and look for the circumstances they
want, and if they can't find them, make them.

George Bernard Shaw
Mrs. Warren's Profession

We live, as we dream—alone.

Joseph Conrad
Heart of Darkness

All that we see or seem
Is but a dream within a dream.

Edgar Allan Poe
A Dream Within a Dream

Everyone is like the moon and has a dark
side which he never shows anybody.

Mark Twain
Following the Equator

Beloved Pan and all ye other gods who haunt this
place, give me beauty in the inward soul, and may
the outward and the inner man be at one.

Socrates
Dialogues, Phaedrus

In the life of each of us, I said to myself, there is
a place remote and islanded, and given to endless
regret or secret happiness.

Sarah Orne Jewett
The Country of the Pointed Firs

To see a world in a grain of sand
And a heaven in a wild flower,
Hold Infinity in the palm of your hand
And Eternity in an hour.

William Blake
Auguries of Innocence

Thanks to the human heart by which we live,
Thanks to its tenderness, its joys, and fears,
To me the meanest flower that blows can give
Thoughts that do often lie too deep for tears.

William Wordsworth
Ode, Intimations of Immortality

No man is an island, entire of itself; every man is a piece of the continent, a part of the main; if a clod be washed away by the sea, Europe is the less, as well as if a promontory were, as well as if a manor of thy friends or of thine own were; any man's death diminishes me, because I am involved in mankind; and therefore never send to know for whom the bell tolls; it tolls for thee.

John Donne
Devotions XVII

The true harvest of my daily life is somewhat as intangible and indescribable as the tints of morning or evening. It is a little star dust caught, a segment of the rainbow which I have clutched.

Henry David Thoreau
Walden

If we had never before looked upon the earth, but suddenly came to it man or woman grown, sat down in the midst of a summer mead, would it not seem to us a radiant vision? The hues, the shapes, the song and life of birds, above all the sunlight, the breath of heaven, resting on it; the mind would be filled with its glory, unable to grasp it, hardly believing that such things could be mere matter and no more. Like a dream of some spirit-land it would appear, scarce fit to be touched lest it should fall to pieces, too beautiful to be long watched lest it should fade away. So it seemed to me as a boy, sweet and new each morning; and even now, after the years that have passed, and the lines they have worn in the forehead, the summer mead shines as bright and fresh as when my foot first touched the grass.

Richard Jefferies
The Open Air

On the plains of Hesitation bleach the bones of
countless millions who, at the dawn of victory, sat
down to wait . . . and waiting, died.

attributed to George Cecil
source unknown

Dreams are the touchstones of our characters.

Henry David Thoreau
*A Week on the Concord and
Merrimack Rivers*

Ideals are like stars; you will not succeed in touching
them with your hands. But like the seafaring man on

the desert of waters, you choose them as your guides,
and following them you will reach your destiny.

Carl Schultz
Address, Faneuil Hall, Boston, April 18, 1859

It is eternity now. I am in the midst of it. It is about me in the sunshine; I am in it, as the butterfly in the light-laden air. Nothing has to come; it is now. Now is eternity; now is the immortal life.

Richard Jefferies
The Story of My Heart

There is no duty we so much underrate as the duty
of being happy.

Robert Louis Stevenson
An Apology for Idlers

Come, fill the Cup, and in the fire of Spring
The Winter garment of Repentance fling:
    The Bird of Time has but a little way
To fly—and Lo! the Bird is on the Wing.

Edward FitzGerald
The Rubáiyát of
Omar Khayyám

Yet Ah, that Spring should vanish with the Rose!
That Youth's sweet-scented Manuscript should close!
The Nightingale that in the branches sang,
Ah whence, and whither flown again, who knows!

Edward FitzGerald
The Rubáiyát of
Omar Khayyám

At Christmas I no more desire a rose
Than wish a snow in May's newfangled mirth.

William Shakespeare
Love's Labour's Lost

Love comforteth like sunshine after rain.

William Shakespeare
Venus and Adonis

A home without a cat—and a well-fed, well-petted
and properly revered cat—may be a perfect home,
perhaps, but how can it prove title?

Mark Twain
Pudd'nhead Wilson

Don't part with your illusions. When they are gone
you may still exist but you have ceased to live.

Mark Twain
Following the Equator

Nothing great was ever achieved without enthusiasm.

Ralph Waldo Emerson
Circles

Life is short, but there is always time for courtesy.

Ralph Waldo Emerson
Social Aims

The only gift is a portion of thyself.

Ralph Waldo Emerson
Gifts

I think I could turn and live with animals,
   they are so placid and self-contain'd,
I stand and look at them long and long.
They do not sweat and whine about their condition…

Not one is dissatisfied, not one is demented
  with the mania of owning things,
Not one kneels to another, nor to his kind that
  lived thousands of years ago,
Not one is respectable or unhappy over the
  whole earth.

Walt Whitman
Leaves of Grass

The finest thing in the world
is knowing how to belong to oneself.

Michel de Montaigne
Of Solitude

If a man does not keep pace with his companions,
perhaps it is because he hears a different drummer.
Let him step to the music which he hears, however
measured or far away.

Henry David Thoreau
Walden

I lived with visions for my company,
Instead of men and women, years ago,
And found them gentle mates, nor thought to know
A sweeter music than they played to me.

Elizabeth Barrett Browning
Sonnets from the Portuguese

Ah, Moon of my Delight who know'st no wane,
The Moon of Heav'n is rising once again:
    How oft hereafter rising shall she look
Through this same Garden after me—in vain!

Edward FitzGerald
The Rubáiyát of
Omar Khayyám

Tasha Tudor

Clues to a unique way of life exist in abundance in Tasha Tudor's art. Candle-lit rooms, food cooked at an open hearth, weaving, and basketmaking find their way into her books, as do children and adults dressed in charming styles of another day. The activities are usually simple—picknicking in a meadow, canoeing in a secluded pond, romping with the corgis, tending to goats and chickens. Friends look through a new book as through a family album. The house in the snow—that's the house in Redding, Connecticut, Tasha knew so well as a child. There's granddaughter Laura on snowshoes, or contemplating the cat. Grandson Winslow it is who hesitates before jumping from the hayloft, or courteously offers a chair to a lady. Nate dreams on a rock. Jenny is seated in the meadow. Jason gathers eggs. Kim, framed by birch trees, studies his image in the water. And Laura, Julie, Winslow, and Jenny enjoy tea with a beloved family friend, Horatio Rabbit. Slyly, the artist even slips herself into a scene here and there, included in a group, or herself as a young mother. And there she is as a child admiring the fragile beauty of water lilies.

Asked how she arrived at a life-style rooted in values and customs of the last century, Tasha Tudor is reticent. It cannot be explained, she replies, other than to say that it is a "state of mind." Pressed further, she speaks of her love of nature, of animals, of nearly lost handcrafts, and particularly of books which have meant much to her. Quotations from some of those books appear in this one. Speaking with "other men's voices," Tasha Tudor reveals—perhaps unwittingly—much of herself.

Many of the quotes have to do with dreams, with nature and animals. These are to be expected. Others call upon solitude as "needful to the imagination." The only true gift, we find, is "a portion of thyself." We also find that there cannot be in a creation—whether it be in a piece of artwork, a gift for a friend, or a well-tended garden—"what in the creator was not."

The wisdom in books exists only "according to the sensibility of the reader." Peace? Nothing can bring it "but yourself." Happiness is "a duty" to self and is found in "minute fractions." As for success—with Thoreau, she greets each day with joy and finds that all nature is her "congratulation."

Perhaps most revealing is a final quotation, from Elizabeth Barrett Browning. Like the poet, Tasha Tudor learned to live with visions for her company. With confidence and determination she has translated those dreams into a life-style which, ultimately, has animated her art. Living a life of loving detail, she speaks of herself as a happy woman.

Good, better, best;
Never rest
Till "good" be "better"
And "better" "best."

Mother Goose